Jay Wilson, Evangelist
1233 N. 8th
Bozeman, MT 59715
Ph: 406-587-8365, 406-586-8061
www.newcreationstudies.org
www.christschurchonline.com
email: wilsonj@mcn.net

Dear Reader.

This study is the second in a series designed to teach you the basics of the New Testament. It is our prayer that it will accomplish its purpose.

The basic conclusions reached in this study are as follows:

1. Our problem is that our own sins condemn us to hell.
2. The good news—the gospel—is that Jesus died for our sins.
3. We answered the question, "What must I do?" and found that we must:
    a) Believe that Jesus is the Christ, and that He was raised from the dead.
    b) Repent.
    c) Confess with the mouth that Jesus is Lord.
    d) Be immersed (in water) into Christ for the forgiveness of our sins.
4. Repentance includes an actual change in behavior.
5. Baptism is immersion in water, and it is essential to salvation. There is only one acceptable immersion—that is immersion into Christ through the medium of water as a result of an individual's own desire to obey the gospel.
6. If a person refuses to do God's will, he will burn forever; if he does God's will, he will live forever!
7. The Christian must remain faithful until death.

We want to stress that the major point in this whole study is that we must come to know God on His terms—not our own—and that His terms are revealed plainly and clearly in the New Testament.

We remind the reader that the author of this booklet is a human being subject to error, ignorance, and misunderstanding. You yourself must study "to see if these things are so."

The New American Standard Version was used in preparation of this study, and is quoted throughout.

Your servant,

Jay Wilson

"The Bible only . . . makes Christians only . . ."

GOD'S PLAN OF SALVATION

Introduction:

a) "I am the way, and the truth, and the life; no one comes to the Father, but through Me" (John 14:6).

b) God now requires that all men obey the gospel (II Thessalonians 1:7-10); ignorance is no excuse (Acts 17:30,31).

Outline:

1. The Problem
2. The Gospel
3. What Must I Do?
4. God's Teaching About Repentance
5. God's Teaching About Baptism
6. The Choice
7. The Need To Overcome

I. The Problem

A. Sin is disobedience to God's commands
   - Genesis 2:17 — God's command: "Do not eat of the fruit of the tree of knowledge of good and evil."
   - Genesis 3:10 — Adam and Eve's disobedience

B. Sin separates man from God
   - Isaiah 59:1,2 — Our sins have separated us from God
   - James 1:13-16 — Separation from God is spiritual death

C. All men have sinned
   - Romans 3:23 — All have sinned
   - Galatians 3:22 — God shut up all men in the jailhouse called sin

D. Small children are innocent and uncondemned
   - Ezekiel 18:20 — No on can inherit another's sin; children therefore cannot inherit Adam's sin
   - Romans 7:9 — There was a time in Paul's life when the Law did not apply; but when the Law took effect, then sin became alive and he died spiritually

E. The penalty for sin is eternal damnation
   - Romans 6:23 — The wages of sin is death
   - Matthew 25:46 — The good go away to eternal life; the bad to eternal punishment
   - Acts 8:24 — The apostles preached about hell and damnation

i

Every man has the problem that his sins, even though they may seem small, separate him from God and condemn him to hell.

II. The Gospel

- Gospel — good story, good news, evangel
- I Corinthians 15:1-5 — Christ died for our sins, was buried, rose again on the third day, and appeared to witnesses
- I Corinthians 5:7 — Christ is our Passover Lamb
- John 19:31-37 — Christ is the perfect sacrifice; He shed His blood for our sins
- Hebrews 9:22 — Without the shedding of blood there is no forgiveness
- Galatians 3:13 — Christ became a curse for us in order to break the curse of the Law that was on us (Hebrews 9:11-14)
- John 3:16 — God's purpose is not to condemn us. He loved us, and sent His only Son to die for us

The good news is that Christ died for our sins just like the Old Testament said He would. Like the Passover lamb of old, Christ shed His blood for the forgiveness of our sins, and so broke the curse of the Law for us. God sent His Son to die for us, then raised Him from the dead.

III. What Must I Do?

- The sign above the cross — Mark 15:26; Luke 23:38; Matthew 27:37; John 19:19,20 — No one verse of scripture gives all the information about the words on the cross; it is necessary to put all the accounts together
- Mark 2:1-12 — Jesus had authority on earth to forgive sins
- Hebrews 9:16,17 — The new covenant began at Christ's death
- Luke 23:39-43 — Jesus forgave the thief on the cross before He died and the new covenant began
- Acts 16:16-34 — The jailer believed and was baptized
- Acts 2:36-38 — On the day of Pentecost they were told to repent and be baptized for the forgiveness of their sins
- Acts 8:26-40 — Confession of the Lord Jesus with the mouth is necessary to salvation (see Romans 10:9,10)
- Acts 22:16 — The apostle Paul was baptized to wash away his sins

The new will of Christ began with His death on the cross. For-giveness of sins under the new covenant is available when you

meet the following conditions:
1. Believe that Christ died for your sins, and that God raised Him from the dead.
2. Repent.
3. Confess with your mouth that Jesus is Lord.
4. Be baptized to wash away your sins.

IV. God's Teaching About Repentance

- Jonah 3:1-10 — When God saw the people's change in behavior, He decided not to destroy Nineveh
- Matthew 12:41 — Jesus said that the change in behavior of the people of Nineveh was repentance
- II Corinthians 7:9-10 — Godly sorrow produces repentance

Repentance is a change in attitude that must result in a change in behavior. If there is no change, there is no repentance.

V. God's Teaching About Baptism

- "baptizo" — means to immerse, submerse, plunge, dip into
- Acts 2:38; Acts 10:47,48 — Immersion in the name of Jesus is in water. It is for the forgiveness of sins.
- Romans 6:1-11 — We are immersed into Christ. We are immersed into the death of Christ where we contact Christ's blood. We are buried with Christ in immersion. Immersion is the likeness of the death, burial, and resurrection of Christ. In that likeness we are planted in union with Christ, crucify the old man, and come forth in the likeness of His resurrection, freed from sin.
- Galatians 3:26,27 — We are sons of God by faith in Jesus. A detail of that faith is that when we were immersed into Christ, we were clothed with Christ. The Father then sees not us, but Jesus, following our immersion into Him.
- I Corinthians 12:13 — We are immersed into the body of Christ
- Colossians 2:12 — We are buried with Christ in immersion, and raised with Him through faith in the working of God.
- Romans 6:17,18 — Immersion is the likeness, or the form (mold) of the basic teaching (doctrine) of Christ — the death, burial, and resurrection of Him. The form of the teaching, immersion, must be obeyed from your own heart, not another's.

- I Peter 3:21 — Immersion saves us by the resurrection of Christ. It is an appeal to God for a clean conscience.
- John 3:3-5 — One must be born of water and Spirit to enter the kingdom of God. Water and Spirit are present at immersion (Acts 2:38).
- Titus 3:5 — Immersion is the washing of regeneration. The Holy Spirit is received in immersion, and He continues to renew the Christian.
- Ephesians 5:25-27 — The church, the body of Christ, has been cleansed by the washing of water. This washing cleanses the bride and begins to make her ready for the marriage to the Lamb (Revelation 19:7-9). This washing is accomplished in connection with the word (I Peter 1:22,23).
- Ephesians 4:4-6 — There is one Lord, one faith, one immersion; not one Lord, many faiths, and many baptisms.

When a person is immersed, God places him into Christ. In this way immersion saves a person by the resurrection of Christ — there he is born again as he is buried with Christ in immersion, to be resurrected with Christ to walk in newness of life. He is regenerated as he receives the Holy Spirit in the washing. There is only one immersion as far as God is concerned — into Christ. God will not recognize any other.

VI. The Choice

- II Thessalonians 1:8-10 — Everyone who does not know Christ, or who does not obey the gospel will be punished when Jesus comes again.
- Revelation 20:15 — Everyone whose name is not in the book of life will be thrown into the lake of fire at judgment.
- Romans 8:9 — Everyone who does not have the Spirit of Christ does not belong to Christ.
- John 3:17-21 — Those who hate the light will not come to Jesus on His terms; those who practice the truth will.
- Matthew 7:21 — It is necessary to do God's will in order to enter the kingdom of heaven.

Every person has a choice — to obey the gospel, or to disobey it. Obedience results in eternal life; disobedience results in eternal punishment.

VII. The Need To Overcome
- Revelation 21:1-8 — We must overcome to inherit heaven.
- Hebrews 6:4-8 — There is a point of "no return."
- II Peter 2:20-22 — A Christian who goes back into the world is in a worse state than he was before he became a Christian.
- Galatians 5:4 — A Christian can fall from grace.
- Revelation 2:10 — A Christian must remain faithful until death to receive the crown of life.

A Christian must remain faithful until death. He must meet obstacles in his path and overcome them.

GOD'S PLAN OF SALVATION

INTRODUCTION

Jesus Christ said, "I am the way, and the truth, and the life; no one comes to the Father but through Me" (John 14:6).

The plain teaching of the Holy Bible is that no man, regardless of race, creed, color, or ethnic background, is going to walk into God's heaven on his own. The only way any person is going to pass through the "pearly gates" is if he has an Advocate with the Father, Jesus Christ the righteous.

At one point in man's existence God made allowance for man's lack of knowledge concerning Him. But since Christ died on the cross, ignorance is no excuse; for as Paul said when he spoke to the people of Athens, "Therefore, having *overlooked* the times of ignorance, God is now declaring to men that all everywhere should repent, because He has fixed a day in which He will judge the world in righteousness through a Man whom He has appointed, having furnished proof to all men by raising Him from the dead" (Acts 17:30,31).

And there will be no mercy for those who do not know, and for those who refuse to obey. ". . . the Lord Jesus shall be revealed from heaven with His mighty angels in flaming fire, dealing out retribution to *those who do not know God* and to *those who do not obey the gospel* of our Lord Jesus" (II Thessalonians 1:7,8).

Since eternity hangs in the balance for us, it is well worth our time to examine God's teaching about salvation—not some man's teaching, not some denomination's teaching, not some church's teaching—but God's teaching revealed in His word, the Bible. In this study we will let God define His own terms, and let Him give us His judgment in such matters. We do not wish to add to—nor subtract from—His teaching, knowing that to do so brings damnation to ourselves.

OUTLINE

Our study will break down into the following seven topics:

1

I. THE PROBLEM

Sin Is Disobedience To God's Commands

Man's problem started way back in the Garden of Eden. God told Adam that he could eat of the fruit of any tree in the garden except one—the tree of the knowledge of good and evil. God told Adam that if he ate from that tree, he would "surely die" (Genesis 2:17).

Adam and Eve's disobedience is recorded in Genesis 3:1-12. From the beginning we note that the serpent's plan of attack has been that God didn't really mean what He said. "And the serpent said to the woman, 'You *surely shall **not** die!*' " (Genesis 3:4).

So Eve was deceived (I Timothy 2:14) by the devil, and Adam and Eve ate. In doing so they sinned. Just as breaking a law or command of men is a crime, so breaking a command of God is sin.

Sin Separates Man From God

God told Adam, "In the day you eat from it [the tree of knowledge of good and evil], you will surely die" (Genesis 2:17). Did Adam die on the day that he ate the forbidden fruit? The Bible says that "all the days that Adam lived were 930 years, and he died" (Genesis 5:5).

Maybe God did lie to Adam? Maybe He was kidding Adam along a little so that Adam wouldn't eat of that fruit?

No! Adam died on the day that he ate of the fruit! He died the kind of death God fears most for His children—*spiritual death!*

The word *death* means "separation." When a person dies physically, the spirit is separated from the body (James 2:26). *Spiritual death* is the separation of the spirit from God, not from the body.

What causes this separation? What dread disease is this that separates a man from the Father of spirits?

Isaiah, speaking for the Lord, tells us: "Behold, the Lord's hand is not so short that it cannot save; neither is His ear so dull that it cannot hear. But your iniquities have made a separation between you and your God, and your sins have hidden his face from you, so that He does not hear" (Isaiah 59:1,2).

That's the problem. A man's sins — S-I-N-S — separate him from God! And, as James said, "Each one is tempted when he is carried away and enticed by his own lust. Then when lust has conceived, it gives birth to sin; and when sin is accomplished, it brings forth death. Do not be deceived, my beloved brethren" (James 1:14-16).

All Men Have Sinned

"Well," you say, "That's all right for somebody else. But I'm not a streetwalker, or rapist, or drug-pusher (or whatever)."

What you are trying to say, friend, is that you don't want to be classed with "sinners." Let God instruct you: "For all have sinned, and fall short of the glory of God" (Romans 3:23); and "If we say that we have not sinned, we make Him a liar" (I John 1:10).

We wouldn't want to call God a liar. So we are forced to admit that we, like the Ephesians of old, are "dead in our trespasses and sins" (Ephesians 2:1), and that we are separated from God.

Why? Why has God so designed the nature of man that we all come out sinners, and inherit a sinner's condemnation? He answers, in Galatians 3:22: "But the Scripture has shut up all men under sin, that the promise by faith in Jesus Christ might be given to those who believe."

God made a jailhouse out of sin, and He used the Scripture to put us all in it. What does every prisoner want more than anything else? He wants out! He wants to hear the clink of the jailer's key in the door, and the voice telling him that he can go free. God has put us in His jailhouse. He knows that when we realize this, we also will want out. And to get out of this jailhouse, there is only ONE WAY! JESUS!!

Small Children

What about children? Are they sinners who are condemned? Are they included in the statement that "all have sinned?" Do children inherit the sin of Adam?

In Ezekiel 18:20, we find this: "The person who sins will die. The son will not bear the punishment for the father's iniquity, nor will the father bear the punishment for the son's iniquity; the righteousness of the righteous will be upon himself, and the wickedness of the wicked will be upon himself." No one can inherit the guilt of another's sin. Because of Adam's sin, death entered the world (Romans 5:12-14), but the eternal reward is based on the individual's own behavior. No one is condemned because he has inherited Adam's sin.

In Romans 7, Paul uses himself as an example. Since God shows no partiality (Romans 2:11), what is true of Paul is true of all men. He says: "And I was once alive apart from the Law; but when the commandment came, sin became alive, and I died" (Romans 7:9). The Law was in existence long before Paul was born. But there was a time in his life when the Law did not apply to him, and he was alive in God's fellowship—even though he probably stole his brother's toys (if he had a brother) and threw dirt at the neighbor children. But there came a time in his life when the Law did apply, and he was now accountable for his sin, and he lost his fellowship with God.

Small children today are like Paul in his infancy. The Law which shuts up men under sin does not apply to children; they are innocent and uncondemned. But when the time comes that the Law applies to their lives (they will know, and God will know, when that time is), then they will be accountable for their sins, and they will also die, losing their fellowship with God. This is what James is speaking of when he says, "But each one is tempted when he carried away and enticed by his own lust. Then when lust has conceived, it gives birth to sin; and when sin is accomplished, it brings forth death" (James 1:14,15).

Of little children, Jesus says, ". . . their angels in heaven continually behold the face of My Father . . ." (Matthew 18:10). To the rest of us He says, ". . . unless you are converted and become like children, you shall not enter the kingdom of heaven" (Matthew 18:3).

4

Children have no need of redemption, unlike the rest of us, for they have not yet lost their fellowship with God. The words of God in the Bible are directed to those who are capable of being responsible for their own actions.

The Penalty For Sin Is Eternal Damnation

What happens, then, if the one who is old enough to be accountable for his sin, and is placed by the Scripture in that jailhouse—what happens if he remains in the jailhouse? Paul answers, "For the wages of sin is death, but the gift of God is eternal life in Christ Jesus our Lord" (Romans 6:23).

Notice that *death* here is contrasted with *eternal life*. The death that Paul is talking about is eternal death—eternal separation from God. Notice furthermore, he speaks of the wages of sin. Wages are something earned, something deserved. We all deserve—we have all earned—the right to burn in hell forever. And if a person stays in the jailhouse of sin until his physical death, he will get what he has earned.

Jesus, in talking of the unrighteous, said, "And these will go away into eternal punishment, but the righteous into eternal life" (Matthew 25:46). Eternal punishment is the opposite of eternal life, and it lasts just as long!

The punishment for sin is eternal damnation. God uses force to persuade human nature that it must take on a new nature. As the Lord said, in referring to Himself as the stone: "And he who falls on this stone, will be broken to pieces; but on whomever it falls, it will scatter him like dust" (Matthew 21:44). We must willingly fall on the Rock of Jesus Christ, and break our will to do the will of our new Master. Either we confess Him as Lord here on earth voluntarily, or we will do it later under force: "Therefore also God highly exalted Him, and bestowed on Him the name which is above every name, that at the name of Jesus every knee should bow, of those who are in heaven, and on earth, and under the earth, and that *every tongue should confess that Jesus Christ is Lord,* to the glory of God the Father" (Philippians 2:9-11).

Many people reject this God who will condemn a man to the black burning recesses of hell forever because of sin. They prefer a god of their own imagination who, as a loving god, could not possibly bear to punish one of His children. These are the days, we are told, when we must "accentuate the positive, and eliminate the negative." Modern thought teaches that we must avoid all mention of sin and hell, and hold forth the good things of God. We must never, never indicate in any way than individual is outside the hearing of God, but that we are all equally His children.

One time I was distributing a tract entitled *"Do You Want To Go To Heaven?"* When you opened the tract, it stated, "As you stand right now, you can't." And it went on to explain how God had placed all men under sin, in order to show mercy to all.

I knocked on the door of an apartment inside an old, old building. A bushy-bearded, red-headed man answered. I handed him the tract and asked him to read it. As soon as he opened it he roared, "All you guys are just the same. You're all negative!"

The apostle Peter was apparently "negative." In Acts 8, he and the apostle John went down to Samaria to the places where Philip the evangelist had been preaching. When they arrived, a converted sorcerer named Simon noticed that they could pass on special powers by the laying-on-of-hands.

He said to them, as he offered them money, "Give to me this authority as well . . ."

"But Peter said to him, 'May your silver perish with you . . . your heart is not right before God. Therefore repent of this wickedness of yours, and pray the Lord that if possible, the intention of your heart may be forgiven you . . .'

"But Simon answered and said, 'Pray to the Lord for me yourselves, so that *nothing of what you have said* may come upon me'" (Acts 8:19-24).

What was it that Peter had said to Simon? We can only guess, regarding the whole detail, but we know that it was something "negative" that terrified Simon the Sorcerer.

6

Modern thinking may say that fear doesn't work. God uses both fear and love to motivate. As He said long ago through wise Solomon: "The fear of the Lord is the beginning of wisdom" (Proverbs 9:10).

Conclusion

You don't solve a problem by avoiding it. And every man has the problem that his sins, even though they may seem small, separate him from God, and condemn him to hell.

II. THE GOSPEL

I Corinthians 15:1-5

Paul wrote to the church at Corinth: "Now I make known to you, brethren, the gospel which I preached to you, which also you received, in which also you stand, by which also you are saved, if you hold fast the word which I preached to you, unless you believed in vain. For I delivered to you as of first importance what I also received, that *Christ died for our sins* according to the Scriptures, and that *He was buried,* and that *He was raised on the third day* according to the Scriptures, and that he *appeared . . .*" (I Corinthians 15:1-5).

Paul said that the Christians were saved by the gospel. What is the gospel? The word *gospel* comes from the Old English words *god* and *spel,* meaning "good" and "story." The gospel is the "good story." The word used in the Greek language—in which the New Testament was written—is *evangel,* which means "good news."

The gospel is good news to us because it tells us how to solve our problem of sin. Paul said that as of first importance was that Christ died for our sins, and that He was buried, and that He rose again on the third day.

GOOD NEWS! CHRIST DIED FOR OUR SINS!

Notice how the Bible operates like an "I've got some good news and some bad news for you" story. First you get the bad news—your sins condemn you to hell. Then you get the good news—Christ died for your sins!

7

The Passover Lamb

Our story begins back in the Old Testament. When God was preparing to bring the people of Israel out of Egypt, He told them to kill a lamb, and sprinkle the blood over the top and sides of the doors of their houses. God was going to kill the first-born male of both man and beast in all the land of Egypt as the last of ten plagues, and He told the Israelites: "And the blood shall be a sign for you on the houses where you live, and when I see the blood I will *pass over* you, and no plague will befall you when I strike the land of Egypt" (Exodus 12:13).

Because God passed over the houses where the blood was sprinkled, it became known as *the Lord's Passover.* Jesus Christ is our Passover Lamb, according to I Corinthians 5:7. Just as death did not enter the homes where the blood of a lamb was sprinkled in Egypt, so death will not enter the life of the one on whom the blood of Jesus has been sprinkled (Hebrews 10:22). This is what John the Baptist meant when he said, "Behold, the Lamb of God who takes away the sin of the world" (John 1:29).

GOOD NEWS! CHRIST WAS SACRIFICED, AS THE PASSOVER LAMB, FOR OUR SINS!

The Perfect Sacrifice

Then God, through Moses, led the people out of Egypt, across the Red Sea and into the Wilderness, where God gave them the Law (including the Ten Commandments) and the priesthood. Part of the Old Testament ritual was the yearly offering of a male goat in atonement for the people's sins on the Day of Atonement (Leviticus 16:1-34).

The sacrifices of the Old Testament merely pointed forward to the sacrifice of the Lamb of God. Since it is impossible for the blood of bulls and goats to forgive sin (Hebrews 10:4), at the right time God sent His first-born Son, without blemish, as the perfect sacrifice, to take away the sins of men of all ages—past, present, and future.

John described the offering of the perfect sacrifice in this way: "The Jews therefore, because it was the day of preparation, so that the bodies should not remain on the cross on the Sabbath (for that Sabbath was a high day), asked Pilate that their legs might be broken, and that they

might be taken away. The soldiers therefore came, and broke the legs of the first man, and of the other man who was crucified with Him; but coming to Jesus, when they saw that He was already dead, they did not break His legs; but one of the soldiers pierced His side with a spear, and immediately *there came out blood and water.* And he who has seen has borne witness, and his witness is true; and he knows that he is telling the truth, so that you also may believe" (John 19:31-35).

GOOD NEWS! CHRIST IS THE PERFECT SACRIFICE, AND SHED HIS BLOOD FOR OUR SINS!

The Significance Of The Shed Blood

In God's scheme of things, blood must always be shed in connection with forgiveness of sins. It was true in the days of Abel, in the days of Abraham, and in the days of Moses. As the writer of Hebrews says, "And according to Law, one may almost say, all things are cleansed with blood, and without the shedding of blood, there is no forgiveness" (Hebrews 9:22).

And now, having shed His blood on the cross, "Christ appeared as a High Priest of the good things to come, [and] He entered through a greater and more perfect tabernacle, not made with hands, that is to say, not of this creation; and not through the blood of goats and calves, but through His own blood, He entered the holy place once for all, having obtained eternal redemption" (Hebrews 9:11,12).

The cross is God's redemption center, where our worthless sins are exchanged for valuable eternal life. "Christ redeemed us from the curse of the Law, having become a curse for us—for it is written, 'Cursed is everyone who hangs on a tree'—in order that in Christ Jesus the blessing of Abraham might come to the Gentiles, so that we might receive the promise of the Spirit through faith" (Galatians 3:13,14). And the blood of the cross, the blood of our redemption, was prefigured by the Old Testament sacrifices, and produces for us clean consciences. "For if the blood of goats and bulls and the ashes of a heifer sprinkling those who have been defiled, sanctify for the cleansing of the flesh, how much more will the blood of Christ, who through the eternal Spirit offered Himself without blemish to God, cleanse your conscience from dead works to serve the living God?" (Hebrews 9:13,14).

GOOD NEWS! CHRIST SHED HIS BLOOD SO THAT WE MIGHT HAVE CLEAN CONSCIENCES!

Summary

God locked up mankind in the jailhouse called sin. But as a loving Father, He did not leave us without hope. "For God so loved the world that He gave His only begotten Son, that whoever believes in Him should not perish, but have eternal life" (John 3:16).

The good news is that Christ died for our sins just as the Old Testament said He would. Like the Passover lamb of old, Christ shed His blood for the forgiveness of our sins, and so broke the curse of the Law. After accomplishing these things in His death, He was raised from the dead to live forever.

III. WHAT MUST I DO?

The Sign On The Cross

Now that we've heard that the gospel is that Christ died for our sins, and that He was buried, and that He rose again, what do we do about it?

Peter and Paul both said that the gospel must be obeyed (II Thessalonians 1:8, I Peter 4:17). To find out how the gospel was obeyed, we are going to examine four conversions of the New Testament. In so doing we will find our answer to the question, "What must I do?".

But first a word of introduction. Sometimes verses or portions of scripture on the surface seem to be contradictory. Consider, for example, the four accounts of the sign above Jesus as He hung on the cross.

10

"And they put up above His head the charge against Him which read, 'THIS IS JESUS THE KING OF THE JEWS.' " (Matthew 27:37).

"And the inscription of the charge against Him read, 'THE KING OF THE JEWS.' " (Mark 15:26).

"Now there was also an inscription above Him, 'THIS IS THE KING OF THE JEWS.' " (Luke 23:38).

"And Pilate wrote an inscription also, and put it on the cross. And it was written, 'JESUS THE NAZARENE, THE KING OF THE JEWS.' Therefore this inscription many of the Jews read, for the place where Jesus was crucified was near the city; and it was written in Hebrew, Latin, and in Greek" (John 19:19,20).

Which one of the four accounts is correct? All four differ.

Some try to handle the problem by stating that each account simply described the sign as the writer saw it, or as he was informed concerning it. Implicit in the Bible's being the Word of God is that not only must each account be from the perspective of the author, but also that each account must be singularly accurate!

Let's go back through and note how the four accounts are individually accurate, different from one another, and yet perfectly consistent.

We'll begin with Mark's account, and note the changes in the succeeding account in italics:

THE KING OF THE JEWS—Mark.
THIS IS THE KING OF THE JEWS—Luke.
THIS IS *JESUS* THE KING OF THE JEWS—Matthew.
JESUS *THE NAZARENE,* THE KING OF THE JEWS *(in Hebrew, Latin, and in Greek)*—John.

Note that this is what the sign said:
THIS IS JESUS THE NAZARENE, THE KING OF THE JEWS (in Hebrew, Latin, and in Greek).

Note also that *none* of the four accounts records the total message of the sign. All four accounts are individually accurate, *but all four must be put together* to have complete information as to what was on the sign.

This illustrates a very important principle in interpreting the Bible. All verses of scripture are accurate, and no one verse may be placed in juxtaposition to another.

For example, to throw out Matthew's account of the lettering on the sign because it is different from John's is a subtle denial that the Bible is the Word of God. "All Scripture is inspired by God and profitable for teaching, for reproof, for correction, for training in righteousness; that the man of God may be adequate, equipped for every good work" (II Timothy 3:16). To say that one verse of scripture is not true "because another verse of scripture says something different" is to place the scripture in opposition to itself. The scriptures do mesh perfectly—any problem is in the mind of the interpreter, and not the Bible.

As we approach the question, "What must I do?", we must keep this principle in mind. To throw out the testimony of the book of Acts "because it is inconsistent with John and Ephesians" is a subtle denial that the Bible is the Word of God, and the characteristic of a stubborn and rebellious mind.

The New Covenant

When the Lord Jesus walked the earth, He forgave the people's sins as He wished. In Mark 2, for example, Jesus forgave a paralyzed man's sins, explaining that "the Son of Man has authority on earth to forgive sins" (Mark 2:10).

But since Jesus' death on the cross, forgiveness of sins can be obtained only in accordance with the terms of His will. The writer of Hebrews explains it to us: "For where a covenant is, there must of necessity be the death of the one who made it. For a covenant is valid only when men are dead, for it is never in force while the one who made it lives" (Hebrews 9:16,17).

In other words, it's just like a rich man's will. While the man is alive, he can pass out one-hundred dollar bills all he wants to. But when he dies, they lock up his estate, and nothing is distributed except as the will designates.

When the will goes to probate court, they read the "last will and testament" of John Doe. In accordance with English common law they

12

use both the Anglo-Saxon word and the Latin word. *Will*—that's the Anglo-Saxon word—that's for the common people. *Testament*—that's the Latin word—that's for the lawyers. *Will, testament,* and *covenant* in this context mean the same things. And that's what our New Testament is—it's the New Will of Christ.

So Jesus had authority to pronounce forgiveness of sins as He desired while He lived. But, once He died, forgiveness of sins is granted only through the terms of His will (or covenant, or testament), revealed to us through the apostles, who were guided into "all truth" through the Holy Spirit (John 16:13).

But for us to find forgiveness of sin, we are going to have to look in the Bible record for examples which took place *after* Christ died on the cross. We are going to have to go to the book of Acts to find what men were told in answer to their question, "What must I do?" And we will find that we will have to study the writings of the apostles and other inspired men in the epistles to find the Lord's will for us today.

God shows no partiality (Romans 2:11). The things which He required from men in the early days of the church are the same as He requires from us now.

The Philippian Jailer

For our first example, let's go to the conversion of the jailer from the city of Philippi, recorded in Acts 16:16-34. The apostle Paul, and a man who worked with him named Silas, were preaching the gospel in this city. There was a certain girl who had an evil spirit in her who kept following after them and saying, "These men are the bond-servants of the Most High God, who are proclaiming to you the way of salvation." This annoyed Paul, so one day he turned around and cast the spirit out of her.

This was the beginning of their troubles. Some men were using the girl's "fortune-telling" abilities to make money for themselves. When the spirit went out of her, their profit scheme went out the window. So they took Paul and Silas to court, and had them jailed on trumped up charges.

Paul and Silas were thrown into the inner prison, which was probably pretty dark, damp, and dingy, and the bugs that made their home in such places probably made their presence known. But at midnight,

13

Paul and Silas were singing hymns and praying. They had what I call PMA—Positive Mental Attitude.

All of a sudden, an earthquake rocked the building, the doors swung open, and the chains dropped from the prisoners' hands and legs. Under normal circumstances, the prisoners would have been leaving the prison like hornets leaving a stirred-up nest. But they didn't—they just stood there.

But the jailer didn't know that. As soon as he was roused from his sleep, he saw the doors of the prison house hanging open. Since in those days the penalty for letting a prisoner escape was to be put to death, he thought he'd get it over quickly, and drew his sword to kill himself.

"But Paul cried out with a loud voice, saying, 'Do yourself no harm, for we are all here.' And he called for lights and rushed in and, trembling with fear, he fell down before Paul and Silas, and after he brought them out, he said, 'Sirs, what must I do to be saved?' "

This man asked the same question we are asking, "What must I do to be saved?" So let's see what Paul and Silas told him.

"And they said, *Believe in the Lord Jesus*, and you shall be saved, you and your household.' "

In answer to his question, they told him that he had to believe in the Lord Jesus. The jailer probably didn't know who Jesus was. This was the first time the gospel had come to these parts, and the man was undoubtedly a pagan. So Paul and Silas told him who Jesus was.

"And they spoke the word of the Lord to him together with all who were in his house."

The Bible says that "faith comes by hearing, and hearing by the word of Christ" (Romans 10:17). The only way anyone can believe in the Lord Jesus is to first hear the word of God preached. This man from Philippi was no exception, and neither was anyone else in the New Testament!

"And he took them that very hour of the night and washed their wounds, and immediately he was baptized, he and his whole household."

Our point of emphasis in this first example is this: In answer to the question, "What must I do?", we find that we must believe in the Lord Jesus. We must believe that He died for our sins, that He was buried, and that He rose again on the third day. Our belief must not be the surface kind of belief where we nod our heads and say, "Okay, I believe you." It must be the kind of belief that is a deep down, crusading conviction. We must believe in our hearts; we must believe with our whole beings.

The Day of Pentecost

Our second example takes place some 15 years earlier than the events in Philippi, and is recorded in Acts 2. This was the first time that the gospel was preached in its completeness. The occasion was the Jewish feast day of Pentecost, just 50 days after Jesus' resurrection from the dead, and just ten days after His ascension into heaven. On this very day every male Jew throughout the world would be in Jerusalem if humanly possible, to observe what was centuries earlier known as the Feast of Weeks, commemorating the beginning of the harvest, and offering up the first fruits to the Lord.

On this day Peter and the rest of the apostles were filled with the Holy Spirit, and stood and preached the death, the burial, and the resurrection of Christ. Peter proved to those listening, by Old Testament scripture, that Jesus was the Messiah, and that He had fulfilled the prophecies exactly.

He said, to the many thousands listening, "Therefore, let all the house of Israel know for certain that God has made Him Lord and Christ—this Jesus whom you crucified" (Acts 2:36)

"Now when they heard this, they were pierced to the heart, and said to Peter and the rest of the apostles, 'Brethren, what shall we do?' " (Acts 2:37)

Peter, speaking by the inspiration of the Holy Spirit, gives us the terms revealed in the New Will of Christ: *"Repent,* and let each of you be baptized in the name of Jesus Christ for the forgiveness of your sins, and you shall receive the gift of the Holy Spirit" (Acts 2:38).

Forgiveness of sins for them (and for us as well), was granted under two conditions: (1) repentance, and (2) baptism in the name of

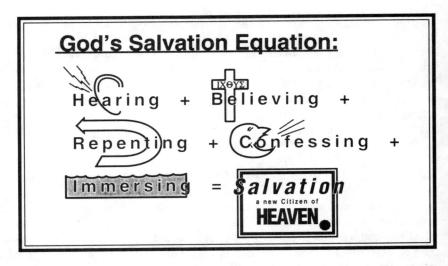

God's Salvation Equation:

Hearing + Believing + Repenting + Confessing + Immersing = *Salvation* a new Citizen of HEAVEN

Jesus Christ. Without repentance, there is no forgiveness of sins. And without baptism in the name of Jesus, there is no forgiveness of sins.

Jesus said, "Unless you repent, you will all likewise perish" (Luke 13:5). Peter said, "God is not willing that any should perish, but that all should come to repentance" (II Peter 3:9).

Our point of emphasis in this second example is this: In answer to the question, "What must I do?", we find that each of us must not only believe in Christ Jesus, but that we must also repent.

The Ethiopian Eunuch

Our third conversion example is found in Acts 8:26-40. Here God sent a preacher named Philip to meet a man from Ethiopia who was on his way back home after he had been to Jerusalem to worship.

The man was riding in his chariot, reading the prophet Isaiah. He didn't understand what he was reading, but Philip did, and beginning with the scripture, he taught the Ethiopian about Jesus. As Philip was explaining things to him they came to some water, and the man wanted to be baptized.

"And Philip said, 'If you believe with all your heart, you may.' And he answered and said, 'I believe that Jesus Christ is the Son of God' " (Acts 8:37). This verse is in the margins of most modern versions of the New Testament, indicating that it is of doubtful authority. However, an examination into the authenticity of this verse will show that it is included in the majority of the ancient reliable texts, and is certainly the word of God. (For an excellent presentation on the reliability of the *majority text*, see the book *Counterfeit Or Genuine*, by David O. Fuller, Grand Rapids International Publications.)

Before Philip would baptize him, he asked the Ethiopian to confess his belief in Jesus. With this other scripture agrees: "If you confess with your mouth Jesus as Lord, and believe in your heart that God raised Him from the dead, you shall be saved; for with the heart a man believes, resulting in righteousness, and with the mouth *confession* is made, resulting in salvation" (Romans 10:9,10)

Our point in this example is this: Not only are belief and repentance required for salvation, but also confession with the mouth that Jesus is Lord.

The Apostle Paul

Our final conversion example is that of Saul of Tarsus, who later became the great apostle Paul. Saul was one of the most violent persecutors of Christians that history has ever known. He was responsible for driving Christians out of the city of Jerusalem shortly after Christ founded the church. And he was very much involved with the death of Stephen, the first Christian martyr.

But one day Saul met with the Lord of the universe, and he changed his attitude. He was on his way to the city of Damascus in what is now Syria to round up Christians there, and bring them back to Jerusalem for trial. Suddenly he was blinded by a bright light, and knocked to the ground. Jesus was dealing with him just like the old Missouri mule—He had to get Paul's attention first. And when the Lord had Paul's attention, He asked him, "Why are you persecuting Me?" (Acts 22:7).

Paul wanted to know who he was talking to, so he asked, "Who are you, Lord?" (The word *Lord* here is an expression of respect much like *Sir,* for example. Paul as yet didn't know that he was speaking to the Lord of lords.) Then the voice answered back, "I am Jesus the Nazarene, whom you are persecuting" (Acts 22:8).

17

Saul wasn't ignorant of whom Jesus the Nazarene was. He had heard Stephen preach about Him. He knew the claims of Christians that Jesus had risen from the dead, and was so proved to be the Son of God. Up to now he had laughed it off. But he wasn't laughing now as he said, "What shall I do, Lord?" (Acts 22:10).

Saul would have done anything that the Lord asked him to do at that point. He would have climbed Mt. Hermon, or run a four-minute mile. The Lord simply told him "Go to Damascus, and there you will be told of all that has been appointed for you to do" (Acts 22:10).

So Saul was led by the hand into Damascus because he was still blind. And he was three days without sight, and neither ate nor drank (Acts 9:8,9).

In the meantime a man named Ananias, a devout man well spoken of by all the Jews, was told by God to go to Saul. And coming in and standing next to Saul, he said, "Brother Saul, receive your sight ... and now why do you delay? Arise, and be baptized, and wash away your sins, calling on His name" (Acts 22:16).

Here was a man, who when he met Jesus on the Damascus Road, *believed* in Him. Here was a man who was *repentant,* as exhibited by his prayer and fasting as he waited to be told what to do. Here was a man who *confessed* with his mouth Jesus as Lord (Acts 22:10). But had his sins been forgiven? The answer is an unqualified **NO!**

The man who was to become the great apostle Paul had to be *baptized* to wash away his sins! God shows no partiality (Romans 2:11). What God required of Paul, He requires of everyone else—rich, poor, black, white, male, or female.

At this point something happens to many people's thinking apparatus. They start asking questions like, "Couldn't God save someone without them being baptized?", or "What if someone was out in the Sahara Desert, and wanted to become a Christian, but died before he could get to the water to be baptized? Would that individual go to hell?"

God has required baptism to wash away sins. And if an individual is in the Sahara Desert, and can't get to the water to be baptized, his sins are going to condemn him to hell.

That, however, is not the point. The Bible says that God is not willing that any should perish (II Peter 3:9). If a man is out in the Sahara Desert and wants to be baptized, God, who would send His only Son to die on the cross for that poor soul in the Sahara Desert, would certainly provide an oasis where the man could be baptized before he died.

My job is to believe, obey, and preach—without question—what God says is necessary for salvation. If I'll do that, God will do the worrying about the black African who has never heard, and the dying man on the Sahara Desert. "So shall My word be which goes forth from My mouth; it shall not return to Me empty, without accomplishing the matter for which I sent it" (Isaiah 55:11).

Summary

In answer to the question, "What must I do?", we have pieced together God's answer from the terms of the New Testament. We must:
1. Believe that Jesus died for our sins, and that God raised Him from the Dead.
2. Repent.
3. Confess with our mouths Jesus as Lord.
4. Be baptized to wash away our sins.

IV. GOD'S TEACHING ABOUT REPENTANCE

Some different ideas

Ask five different people what *repent* means and you'll probably get five different answers. For example, I've heard of a church somewhere whose definition of repentance is such that every year at "Easter time," the members of the congregation climb 2000 concrete stairs to repent for the sins they have committed during the last year.

In contrast, I know people who get smashing drunk on Saturday night, then on Sunday cry a few crocodile tears, and say, "I'm sorry, God." And next Saturday night they go out and do the same thing. And that's their definition of repentance.

19

What's God's definition of repentance? Jesus said, "Unless you repent, you will all likewise perish" (Luke 13:3). If repentance is that important, we had better know what God means by it.

God gives an excellent example of repentance through the city of Nineveh. The Lord told Jonah the prophet, "Arise, go to Nineveh the great city, and cry against it, for their wickedness has come up to Me" (Jonah 1:2). But Jonah jumped aboard a ship headed in the opposite direction instead and was eventually thrown overboard, and swallowed by the great fish.

When the fish spit Jonah up on land, he "hightailed it" for Nineveh. "Now the word of the Lord came to Jonah a second time, saying 'Arise, go to Nineveh the great city and proclaim to it the proclamation which I am going to tell you.'" (Jonah 3:1-3). So Jonah arose and went to Nineveh according to the word of the Lord.

"Then Jonah began to go through the city one day's walk; and he cried out and said, 'Yet forty days and Nineveh will be overthrown'" (Jonah 3:4).

The result of Jonah's preaching was that the people of Nineveh believed God, and took His warning seriously. The king issued a proclamation: ". . . and let men call on God earnestly that each may turn from his wicked way and from the violence which is in his hands. Who knows, God may turn and relent, and withdraw His burning anger so that we will not perish" (Jonah 3:8,9).

"When God saw their deeds, that they turned from their wicked way, then God relented concerning the calamity which He had declared He would bring upon them. And He did not do it" (Jonah 3:10).

Notice that God did not change His mind until He saw their *deeds!*

Matthew 12:41

Jesus said of the people of Nineveh, "The men of Nineveh shall stand up with this generation at the judgment, and shall condemn it, because they repented at the preaching of Jonah; and behold, something greater than Jonah is here" (Matthew 12:41). This is Jesus' definition of repentance—a change in behavior.

Many people have the concept that repentance is sorrow for past mistakes. Paul makes it clear that this is not the case: "For sorrow that is according to the will of God produces a repentance with regret; but the sorrow of the world produces death" (II Corinthians 7:10).

Judas Iscariot was sorry for what he had done, but did not repent—he went out and hanged himself (Matthew 27:3-5). Peter denied the Lord, but repented and lived.

Sorrow *produces* repentance. Mere sorrow is not repentance.

From the Bible we conclude that repentance is a change in attitude that must result in a change in behavior. If there is no change, there is no repentance.

V. GOD'S TEACHING ABOUT BAPTISM

Controversy

If there is any subject in the Bible that is full of controversy and confusion, *baptism* is it. Every denominational group in the world even remotely connected with Christianity practices some variation of baptism. But they all have different forms and different reasons.

Why so much controversy? I think the old farm pond that was near my parents' house holds the answer. In the bottom of this pond—which was dug in the ground to supply gravel for a road built in the 1930's—was a six-inch accumulation of mud. You could play games in this mud—games like "hide the penny." If someone started getting too close to finding the penny, you could always stir up the mud. It would form a cloud so thick that nobody could find anything, and everybody would give up trying to find the penny.

That's what has happened with baptism. Because in baptism an individual's sins are washed away—because baptism unites a person with Christ—the devil is doing his very best to muddy the water so that you don't find the truth, and you just plain give up trying.

I have seen tracts with the title, "What the _____ church

teaches about baptism." It doesn't really matter what any group teaches about baptism. The only thing that really counts is what God teaches about baptism.

Baptizo

The New Testament was written in Greek, because that was the common language of the time, much as English is a somewhat universal language today. There are three Greek words we need to discuss in connection with baptism: *baptizo, rantizo,* and *cheo.*

Baptizo means to immerse, to dip into, to plunge into, to submerge.
Rantizo means to sprinkle.
Cheo means to pour.

Over the years "baptize" has come to mean "to sprinkle, to pour, or to immerse." This is a result of man's tradition, and not God's revelation. When God wrote the New Testament, He always used *baptizo* to describe what we call baptism, never *rantizo* or *cheo.*

It was not until 1311 A.D.—nearly 1300 years after the beginning of Christ's Church—that the Roman Catholic Church, at the Council of Ravenna, Italy, declared sprinkling and pouring to be of equal standing with immersion. And many Protestant churches, such as the Lutheran, Episcopal, and Presbyterian Churches, simply adopted the Catholic practice of sprinkling without checking further into the scriptures.

Since that time Bible translators have always ducked the question of what *baptizo* means. Instead of translating it, they transliterate it—*baptizo* in Greek becomes *baptize* in English, and you figure out for yourself what it means.

God said *immerse* as clearly as He could say it in the Greek language. He said *baptizo.*

Another way to find out the meaning of a word is the way it is used in context. For example, if I ask you to go to the barn, and bring me my saddle, my bridle, and my horse, you know that I am asking you to bring my saddle horse. But if I ask you to go to the shop, and bring me my hammer, my saw, and my horse, don't bring me my saddle horse. Bring me my saw horse. The context dictates what kind of "horse" I am talking about.

Similarly, the context will dictate the meaning of baptize. John the Baptist was baptizing at Aenon near Salim, "because there was much water there" (John 3:23). You don't need much water if you're sprinkling or pouring, but you need much water—two or three feet deep at least—to immerse.

After Jesus was baptized, He "went up immediately from the water" (Matthew 3:16). You don't need to go up from the water unless you've been down in it, as in immersion. In Acts 8:38, Philip and the Ethiopian *both* went down into the water—for sprinkling or pouring,

REQUIREMENTS OF NEW TESTAMENT BAPTISM

New Testament Baptism Requires	Sprinkling Requires	Pouring Requires	Immersion Requires
Water, Acts 10:47	X	X	X
Much water, John 3:23		X(?)	X
Going to the water, Matt. 3:13			X
Administered in water, Mk. 1:9			X
Down into water, Acts 8:38			X
Coming up out of water, Matt. 3:16			X
A burial, Romans 6:4			X
A resurrection, Colossians 2:12			X
Bodies washed, Hebrews 10:22			X

(Taken from Gareth Reese's commentary on the book of Acts)

you both can stand on the edge of the pool and get the job done without either of you having to go down into the water. The context of the scripture dictates immersion.

It is clear from the Bible that God speaks of baptism as being immersion; and from this point on, immersion is what we mean if we say baptism.

Acts 2:38

Acts 2:38 is a scripture verse that we want to cover in some detail. This is a statement which Peter made in response to several thousand Jews' question, "What shall we do?" Peter's answer is: "Repent, and let each of you be immersed in the name of Jesus Christ for the forgiveness of your sins, and you shall receive the gift of the Holy Spirit."

Peter's answer is straight-forward, and contains two require-ments: (1) Repent; and (2) Be immersed in the name of Jesus for the forgiveness of sins.

Nobody, as a rule, gets "hung up" on the necessity of repentance as a requirement for salvation. Immersion in the name of (by the authority of) Jesus for the purpose of forgiveness of sins is where some people have real problems.

Most of the so-called "fundamental evangelical" denominations (Baptist, Pentecostal, etc.) teach that an individual is saved by "faith alone." "For by grace you have been saved through faith; and that not of yourselves, it is the gift of God; not as a result of works, that no one should boast" (Ephesians 2:8,9). Arbitrarily assigning to immersion the status of works, and excluding immersion from faith, such groups automatically come to the conclusion that immersion cannot possibly have anything to do with salvation. Immersion must be a work which follows salvation. Therefore immersion could not possibly be for the purpose of forgiveness of sins—forgiveness would have taken place earlier when the individual was "saved." Therefore, groups which hold this doctrinal position try to squirm around the obvious meaning of Acts 2:38 rather than let God give His definition of faith.

One of the arguments that is used is this: the word translated *for* can also mean *because*. A man is thrown in jail *for* the commission of a crime—he is thrown in jail *because he committed it.* Parallel reason-ing then applies to Acts 2:38; a man is immersed *for* the remission (forgiveness) of sins—a man is immersed *because* his sins are remit-ted (forgiven).

Unfortunately, that attempt to wiggle away from the force of Acts 2:38 will not succeed. The word translated *for* is the Greek word *eis*, which rarely ever means *because,* and certainly not in this context. Consider Matthew 26:28. In this verse, where Jesus is instituting the Lord's Supper, He describes His blood as being shed "for the forgive-ness of sins." Nobody who believes that the Bible is the Word of God would claim that Jesus shed His blood "because mankind's sins were already forgiven." Jesus' blood was shed for the purpose of forgiving men's sins! And that same purpose, in exactly the same language (in Greek as well as in English) is ascribed to immersion!!

Others, still attempting to deny the obvious meaning of Acts 2:38, use a different tack. They say, "Okay, I agree that immersion in the name of Jesus is for the forgiveness of sins. The word *baptizo* means simply to immerse. How do you know that it's referring to immersion in water? Couldn't it be immersion in the Spirit, which occurs when you accept Jesus into your heart—to be followed with water immersion later?"

It could be. But let's look a little deeper into the matter of immersion in Jesus' name. In Acts 8:36, as Philip preached Jesus to the Ethiopian, the eunuch said, "Look! Water! What prevents me from being immersed?" Water immersion evidently has something to do with the preaching of Jesus.

In Acts 10:44, the household of a Gentile (non-Jew) soldier named Cornelius received what the Bible calls the "immersion in the Holy Spirit." This sign from heaven consisted of a sound like a mighty wind, tongues like fire coming down on their heads, and speaking in foreign languages. The sign in this case was for the purpose of convincing the Jewish Christians that Gentiles were acceptable to God, and could be saved. (For more detail, see the study entitled *The Holy Spirit,* the section concerning the immersion in the Holy Spirit.) As a result of this happening, Peter and the Christian men with him were amazed, and Peter said, "'Surely no one can refuse the *water* for these to be immersed who have received the Holy Spirit just as we did, can he?' And he ordered them to be *immersed in the name of Jesus Christ*" (Acts 10:47,48).

Acts 10:47,48 prove beyond any shadow of doubt that immersion in the name of Jesus takes place in water.

Acts 2:38 plainly says, then, that repentance and immersion in water are necessary for salvation, and that immersion in water in Jesus' name is for the forgiveness of sins.

Romans 6:1-11

Romans 6:1-11 is the longest section of scripture in the New Testament dealing with immersion. In the fifth chapter Paul has been writing concerning the greatness of God's grace. The Christian may have a tendency to take advantage of God's willingness to overlook mistakes by deliberately sinning.

The question under discussion is: "Are we to continue in sin that grace might increase?" The answer comes, "May it never be!" followed by a discussion of how we as Christians died to sin.

1. "Or do you not know that all of us who have been immersed into Christ have been immersed into His death?" It is important to note that only in Jesus is there no condemnation (Romans 8:1)! All of God's blessings are reserved for those *in* Jesus (Ephesians 1:3). The most important practical question for every person is: "How do I get **into** Jesus?" This verse of scripture gives God's answer to us—everyone must be **IMMERSED INTO CHRIST JESUS!**

   No one enters into Christ by "accepting Jesus into his heart." This is purely man-made perversion of the gospel—anathema to the Lord, and to be so for us as well (Galatians 1:6-10).

   The only way through the door of salvation is immersion into Jesus! Anyone who tries to enter another way is a thief and a robber (John 10:1).

   When an individual is immersed into Christ, he is immersed into Christ's death. It was in Christ's death that His blood was shed for the forgiveness of our sins (John 19:31-37). When we are immersed into Christ's death we contact the blood which washes away our sins. This is entirely consistent with the teaching of Acts 2:38: "Be immersed . . . for the forgiveness of your sins;" and Acts 22:16: "Be immersed, and wash away your sins."

2. "Therefore, we have been buried with Him through immersion into death, in order that as Christ was raised from the dead through the glory of the Father, so we too might walk in newness of life" (Romans 6:4).

   This is as clear a description of being "born again" as it is possible to write. (See John 3:3). We have been buried with Him in immersion, and resurrected to walk in newness of life. You bury the old man, and a new one is raised who walks in a different life. That's what it means to be "born again." No where does the Holy Spirit even hint that immersion is a "symbol of the conversion that has already taken place." He insists that the process of being born again, in which **He** does the work, is accomplished in immersion.

3. "For if we have become united with Him in the likeness of His death, certainly we shall be also in the likeness of His resurrection" (Romans 6:5)

There is only one Biblical thing that is the likeness of Jesus' death, burial, and resurrection—immersion in water. Sprinkling is not that likeness, neither is pouring. Because this whole section of scripture is dealing with immersion into Christ, this description of immersion into Christ as the likeness of Jesus' death, burial, and resurrection makes it clear that immersion into Christ occurs in water!

Our union with Christ occurs in the likeness of His death—not before, not after—**IN!**

If we have been united with Christ in the likeness of His death, Paul says that we *certainly* shall be in the likeness of His resurrection. An examination of the verse by itself would lead one to think that the primary meaning of the text is that we will be resurrected when Christ comes again. In context, however, the Holy Spirit is talking about a resurrection like Christ's for us in this present age! We have buried the old man; the new man *certainly* is as Christ was after He was resurrected!

4. "... knowing this, that our old self was crucified with Him, that our body of sin might be done away with, that we should no longer be slaves to sin; for he who has died is freed from sin" (Romans 6:6,7).

The biggest problem that a Christian faces is the desire of the flesh to sin. The Christian really needs to be conscious of the fact that the sinful body has been crucified in immersion; it's dead. Therefore a Christian is not a slave to sin—sin has no business telling him what to do. The Christian can tell sin to "get lost;" he is free from sin's power.

5. "Now if we have died with Christ we believe that we shall also live with Him, knowing that Christ, having been raised from the dead, is never to die again; death no longer is master over Him" (Romans 6:8,9).

When Christ was resurrected the devil had no more that he

could do to Him. Christ had destroyed him who had the power of death (Hebrews 2:14). And we believe that we live with Him—"He who hears My words, and believes Him who sent Me, *has* eternal life, and shall not come into judgment, but *has* passed out of death into life" (John 5:24).

6. "For the death that He died, He died to sin, once for all, but the life that He lives, He lives to God. Even so consider yourselves to be dead to sin, but alive to God in Christ Jesus" (Romans 6:10,11).

When Jesus burst forth from the grave, Satan could no longer tempt Him. No longer would the devil be able to meet Him in the wilderness and tempt His flesh with appeals to the lust of the flesh, the lust of the eye, and the boastful pride of life. Sin could no longer touch Him or tempt Him.

We, as a result of our sharing in Christ's death, burial, and resurrection through immersion, are to consider ourselves just as removed from the power of sin as Jesus was when He burst forth from the grave! If we don't think of ourselves as being this way, it's a cinch that we won't even come close to acting that way.

7. The important points in this section are:
    1) Immersion places one into Christ.
    2) A person buries his old man in immersion, and is raised to walk in newness of life—he is born again!
    3) Union with Christ takes place in the likeness of His death, which is immersion in water.
    4) Following immersion into Christ, a Christian is to consider himself just as removed from the power of sin as Jesus was when He was resurrected.

Galatians 3:26,27

In Galatians 3:26,27 we find that Christians are the sons of God through faith in Christ Jesus because everyone who has been immersed into Christ has been clothed with Christ. "For you are all sons of God through faith in Christ Jesus. For all of you who were immersed into Christ have clothed yourselves with Christ."

Once again, the expression "immersed into Christ" is used. As we pointed out in our commentary on Romans 6:3, the only way into Christ is by being immersed into Him. No scheme that man might devise will place a lost and damned-to-hell sinner into Christ.

Many religious groups have trouble reconciling the statement that Christians are sons of God by faith, and that the adoption occurs during immersion into Christ.

Ephesians 2:8,9 states: "For by grace you have been saved through faith; and that not of yourselves, it is a gift of God; not as a result of works, that no one should boast."

Those groups which believe that an individual is saved by "faith alone" define faith as a mental state of mind, involving the belief that Jesus is the Son of God, and trusting Him "totally" for salvation. Under this definition of faith, immersion must be a *work* that *follows* that trust in God, and therefore cannot be connected with salvation, for salvation comes "not as a result of works."

But why not, as in the case with repentance, let God define what He means by "faith"?

In Galatians 3:26, the Holy Spirit tells us that we are sons of God by faith in Christ Jesus. Then He goes on to tell us how that marvelous transition occurred: when we were immersed into Christ, we were clothed with Christ.

For example, suppose that you were going to a costume party. Before you go, you put on a costume that looks like Donald Duck. You have now been clothed with Donald Duck. When someone looks at you, they can't see you—all they can see is the costume.

So it is with immersion into Christ. When you are immersed into Christ, you become clothed with Christ—you have put on a costume that looks exactly like Christ. When God looks at you He sees Jesus—and that is why He accepts you as a son of God; you become sons of God through faith, *because* in being immersed into Christ we have been clothed with Him.

Faith, then, in God's definition, includes more than "simple belief." It includes repentance, confession with the mouth that Jesus is Lord, and immersion in water into Christ.

"For by one Spirit we were all immersed into one body, whether Jews or Greeks, whether slaves or free, and we were all made to drink of one Spirit" (I Corinthians 12:13). There are two possible interpretations of this verse. One is that through the action of the Holy Spirit we have all entered the body of Christ (which is God's church—Ephesians 1:22,23) by being immersed into it. The second is: The word translated *Spirit* is the Greek word *pneuma*. In the original manuscripts all the letters were capitals—there is no way to tell whether *pneuma* is to be translated *Spirit* or *spirit*—only the context will tell. The word *spirit* refers to either our inner person, or an attitude. In other words, another way to translate I Corinthians 12:13 is: "For with one attitude we were all immersed into one body . . ." This alternate translation seems to be more consistent with the scripture's teaching of the repentant sinner making his appeal to God in immersion. (There are some who twist this passage to speak of being baptized in the Holy Spirit. Baptism in the Holy Spirit occurred only twice—once to begin the church on Pentecost, and once to extend salvation to the Gentiles. For more information see the study entitled *The Holy Spirit*.)

There is really no question that immersion into the body occurs through the medium of water, for one cannot be in the body of Christ without being immersed—in water—into Christ.

Colossians 2:12

In this verse the point is again made that we have been buried with Christ in immersion. Here Paul adds to our knowledge by pointing out that from immersion we were "raised up with Him through faith in the working of God, who raised Him from the dead" (Colossians 2:12). Any works connected with immersion are on God's part—we are saved through faith in *His* working!

Romans 6:17,18

Romans 6:17,18 are interesting verses. Although they do not mention immersion directly, they add to our knowledge of the subject.

"But thanks be to God that though you were slaves of sin, you became obedient from the heart to that form of teaching to which you were committed, and having been freed from sin, you became slaves of righteousness" (Romans 6:17,18).

"Having been freed from sin" tips us off that Paul is still talking about immersion, as he was earlier in the chapter (Romans 6:1-11). And that brings to our mind some questions.

The fact that we were obedient from the heart to the *form* of the teaching (or doctrine) to which we were committed, and in that way we were freed from sin, prompts us to ask, "What is the form of doctrine to which we were committed?" The word *form* means "mold" or "likeness." For example, when contractors lay the foundation for a house, the first thing they do is to build "forms." When the forms are completed, concrete is poured into them. When the concrete has set, the forms are ripped off, leaving a concrete foundation. Notice that the forms are not the foundation—they are a *mold* or *likeness* of the foundation.

Christians have obeyed from their hearts something that is a *form* of the doctrine. What is the basic doctrine about Christ? Paul says that he delivered to the Corinthians, as of first importance, "that Christ died for our sins according to the Scriptures, and that He was buried, and that He was raised on the third day according to the Scriptures" (I Corinthians 15:3,4). The basic doctrine is the death, burial, and resurrection of Christ. Is there anything that is the *form* of the doctrine? Is there anything that is the *likeness* of the death, burial, and resurrection of Christ? There certainly is—immersion into Christ! And it is consistent with the rest of the Bible in that obeying the form of the doctrine, we were made free from sin.

One other item—notice that the "form of the teaching to which we were committed" is to be obeyed from **our own hearts!** If a person has been immersed for any reason other than his own desire to obey, his immersion is not meeting the requirements of the Bible. It is easy to see, for example, that infant sprinkling is not valid—no baby obeys from his own heart.

I Peter 3:21

I Peter 3:21 states, that as water served to destroy the old world

31

in Noah's time (II Peter 3:5,6) by immersion in water, and to save Noah and his family, so immersion now saves us. "And corresponding to that, immersion now saves you—not the removal of the dirt from the flesh, but an appeal to God for a good conscience—through the resurrection of Jesus Christ" (I Peter 3:21).

"... immersion now saves you ..." That seems like a pretty plain statement. Those who deny that immersion has anything to do with salvation have real trouble with this verse. Dr. Kenneth Taylor, a Baptist, in his paraphrase of the Bible (the *Living Bible*), gives us his opinion in this way: "That, by the way, is what baptism *pictures* for us; in baptism we show that we *have been saved . . .*" (I Peter 3:21, emphasis added). This is straight Baptist doctrine! Baptists teach that an individual is saved by "accepting Jesus into your heart," and that immersion is a public witness that "you have already been saved."

The Bible, in contrast, teaches that "Immersion now *saves you*—not the removal of dirt from the flesh, but an appeal to God for a good conscience—through the resurrection of Christ."

There are many things that save a person: grace saves, faith saves, the blood of Jesus saves, God saves, obedience saves. If God chooses to make all of these operative when an individual is immersed into Christ, who can set aside that choice?

It is important to note that immersion is an appeal to God for a "good conscience." A good, or clean, conscience has only been available since Christ's death on the cross. Because it is "impossible for the blood of bulls and goats to take away sins" (Hebrews 10:4), even the righteous men of the Old Testament never had the sense of complete forgiveness available through the sacrifice of Christ. They lived during the time in which "both gifts and sacrifices [were] offered which cannot make the worshiper perfect in conscience, since they relate only to food and drink and various washings . . ." (Hebrews 9:9,10).

Immersion is that appeal to God for a clear conscience, and through immersion, a person is saved because he enters the resurrection of Christ.

John 3:3,5

In John 3:3 Jesus told a very important Pharisee named Nicodemus that, "Unless one is born again, he cannot see the kingdom of God." Nicodemus then asked how a person could be born again after he was old. Jesus told him how: "Unless one is born of water and Spirit, he cannot enter into the kingdom of God" (John 3:5).

Being *born again* consists of being born of water and Spirit. Although the passage can be strained to be interpreted in a number of ways, it seems clear that Jesus was speaking of immersion in His name, which clearly includes water and Spirit (Acts 2:38). The kingdom of God did not come until the day of Pentecost following Jesus' resurrection (see the study on the kingdom of God in the lesson entitled *Christ's Church*), neither did God's Spirit (John 7:37-39), and neither did immersion in Christ's name. Jesus was teaching Nicodemus of things yet to come from his standpoint in time; all of these things did come on the same day some $2\frac{1}{2}$ years later.

Titus 3:5

The same point is made in Titus 3:5: "He saved us, not on the basis of deeds which we have done in righteousness, but according to His mercy, by the washing of regeneration and renewing by the Holy Spirit." Paul speaks of God saving us through the *bath* of regeneration. This more literal rendering of the Greek ties together with the thoughts expressed in I Peter 3:21 and John 3:5. Titus 3:5 is clearly speaking of being born again through immersion in water—born of water and Spirit. The *bath* of regeneration eliminates all past sin; the continuing renewing action of the Spirit continues to save the faithful Christian.

Ephesians 5:26

In Ephesians 5:26 Paul speaks of the church as having been "cleansed . . . by the washing of water with the word." Literally the church has been cleansed with the *bath* of water with the word. The word of God cleanses the church, on an individual basis, in immersion. Not mentioning either water or Spirit, but in remarkable unity with the rest of the scriptures, Peter says, ". . . you have been born again . . . through the living and abiding word of God" (I Peter 1:23).

Ephesians 4:4-6

Our final scripture verses dealing with immersion as taught in God's word are Ephesians 4:4-6. In making a plea for the church at Ephesus to preserve the unity of the Spirit, Paul says, "There is one body and one Spirit, just as you also were called in one hope of you calling; one Lord, one faith, one immersion, one God and Father of all who is over all and through all and in all."

Just as there is only one Spirit, and only one Lord, and only one Father, so also there is only one body, and only one faith, and only one immersion.

I have gone into the hospital to visit the patients. I am often asked, "What faith are you?" When I reply, "Christian," the question often comes, "I know. But what faith Christian?"

THERE IS ONLY ONE FAITH—CHRISTIAN!

Similarly there is only one immersion. Denominations practice all their various forms of "baptism" for all their various reasons. As far as God is concerned, there is only *one* immersion—into Christ! Those who have been "baptized" with another "baptism" have wasted their time. They are still lost and condemned to hell by their own sins.

A Few Extraneous Thoughts

One time I telephoned a contact to see if I could drop in and visit for a few minutes. One of the girls answered the phone and said, "Sure, come on out." When I got there, not only was the family there, but also two Baptist preachers. And the preachers were going through their "plan of salvation" with this family.

So I listened quietly as they explained how God loved these people, but that their sins separated them from God, so it became necessary for Jesus to die on the cross for their sins. When the family understood that, the preachers asked them if they would "accept Jesus into their hearts as their personal Savior." At that point I broke in and asked, "What about baptism?" And one of the preachers quoted I Corinthians 1:14: "I thank God that I baptized none of you except Crispus and Gaius." Then he jumped down to verse 17: "For Christ did not send me to baptize, but to preach the gospel." And he proceeded to explain

There is . . . Body Spirit Hope Lord Faith Immersion GOD & FATHER

to me that immersion had nothing to do with salvation—there were a lot of saved people in Corinth, but only Crispus and Gaius, and the household of Stephanus had been immersed.

Knowing what I knew about immersion, I knew that his thinking couldn't be right, but at that time I didn't know how to answer him. ("Let your speech always be with grace, seasoned as it were, with salt, so that you might know how you should answer each person"—Colossians 4:6). So I went home and studied my Bible.

Why did Paul say that he was thankful that he hadn't immersed many in Corinth? He gives the answer himself: ". . . that no one should say you were immersed in *my* name" (I Corinthians 1:15). It wasn't that the Corinthians weren't immersed, because Paul would say later in the same letter, "we were *all immersed* into one body" (I Corinthians 12:13). In Corinth Paul preached the gospel, and let others do the immersing!

One other time I was talking with a gentleman about immersion into Christ. He mentioned that there were more than one hundred scriptures which talk about how a person is saved by faith, but how there were only just a few which mentioned immersion in connection with salvation. Therefore, because immersion wasn't mentioned very often, it wasn't very important. Notice that if that line of reasoning is correct, being born again isn't important at all, because it is mentioned only four times (John 3:3,7; I Peter 1:3,23).

Summary of God's Teaching Concerning Immersion

When a person is immersed, God places him into Christ. In this way immersion saves him by the resurrection of Christ—there he is born again as he is buried with Christ to be resurrected to walk in newness of life. He is regenerated as he receives the Holy Spirit in the washing. There is only one immersion as far as God is concerned—into Christ. God will not accept any other.

VI. THE CHOICE

Many people do not choose to serve God in God's way because God's way is not made clear to them or the consequences of their choice is not made clear to them. In the above section I hope I have made God's way clear. I hope in this following section to make the consequence of choosing not to serve God clear.

II Thessalonians 1:8-10

In II Thessalonians 1:8-10, Paul points out that when Jesus returns, He is going to deal out "retribution to those who do not know God, and to those who do not obey the gospel of our Lord Jesus. And these will pay the penalty of eternal destruction, away from the presence of the Lord and from the glory of His power, when He comes to be glorified in His saints on that day . . ."

It is plain that punishment is going to be meted out, and that the punishment is going to be eternal destruction (a condition of extreme anguish) away from the presence of the Lord. The punishment is coming upon two groups of people:
1. Those who do not know God.
2. Those who do not obey the gospel of our Lord Jesus Christ.

The natives of the African jungles, the Chinese behind the Bamboo Curtain, and the dwellers of American city slums are all destined to burn forever if they do not know God. And all the people who fill the pews in Catholic churches, in Protestant churches, and in Jewish synagogues are destined to burn in hell forever unless they obey the gospel by repenting of their sins and by being immersed into Christ. God requires that we both know Him, and obey His gospel.

Revelation 20:15

Revelation 20:15 states: "And if anyone's name was not found written in the book of life, he was thrown into the lake of fire." How do you get your name written in the Lamb's book of life? The Bible does not state explicitly, but we can make a good guess that your name is written there when you are born again. And if you refuse to be born of water and Spirit, then it's the lake of fire for you.

Romans 8:9

"But if anyone does not have the Spirit of Christ, he does not belong to Him." Unless an individual has repented and been immersed in the name of Jesus, he does not have the Holy Spirit (Acts 2:38. For more detail see the study *The Holy Spirit*.). This is true regardless of how sincere he is in what he believes, how moral and upstanding he is, how much he loves his children, or any other consideration. Unless he has received the Holy Spirit by being immersed into Christ, Christ does not recognize him at all.

John 3:17-21

The question comes to mind: why do many good, moral, religious people refuse to yield themselves to God's plan of salvation? In John 3:20 comes the answer: "For everyone who does evil hates the light, and does not come to the light lest his deeds should be exposed." If a person refuses to see things God's way, God's word is designed to separate him from the Christian (see Hebrews 4:12,13).

Am I saying that anyone who refuses to repent and be immersed for the forgiveness of sins is evil? I'm not saying that. Jesus said that!

And remember, man only looks at the outward appearance—God looks at the heart (I Samuel 16:7).

In contrast, "he who practices the truth comes to the light, that his deeds may be manifested as having been wrought in God" (John 3:21). Sincere people from all backgrounds, cultures, and ages will come to Jesus when the truth of the gospel is presented to them, and they will not rebel at the terms of His plan of salvation. Neither will they stiffen their necks at the demands which He makes on them following their entrance into Christ.

Matthew 7:21

Finally, I ask this question: "Does a person have to do exactly what God says in order to enter the kingdom of heaven (which is the body of Christ, and its eternal habitation)?" Another way of asking the same question is: "What if a person is sincerely doing the best he knows how but he, for example, has been sprinkled instead of immersed? Will he be saved?" Let Jesus answer the question: "Not everyone who says to Me, 'Lord, Lord,' will enter the kingdom of heaven, but he who *does* the will of My Father who is in heaven" (Matthew 7:21). In order to enter the kingdom of heaven, you have to do the will of God. Doing what you think is right will not get you into heaven; you have to do what God thinks is right!

Summary

This is your choice (and mine)—obey or disobey the gospel. Obedience results in eternal life; disobedience results in eternal death.

VII. THE NEED TO OVERCOME

Over the years there have been many discussions as to whether a Christian can lose his salvation. We will, as on other sections, let God answer through His sufficient word—the Bible.

Revelation 21:1-8

After giving us a comforting picture of the love and fellowship in heaven after we, as the bride of Christ, have been made ready, John carries us on into a warning from Him who sits on the throne: "I will give to the one who thirsts from the spring of the water of life without

38

cost. He who overcomes shall inherit these things, and I will be his God and he will be My son. But for the cowardly and unbelieving and abominable and murderers and immoral person and sorcerers and idolaters and all liars, their part will be in the lake that burns with fire and brimstone, which is the second death" (Revelation 21:6).

The test of trust is obedience. If a person trusts Jesus for his salvation, these abominable qualities will be left behind. But if the Christian continues to practice these following his immersion into Christ, or if he slips into them later, his part will be in the lake of fire.

Hebrews 6:4-8

The writer of Hebrews warns us: "For in the case of those who have once been enlightened and have tasted of the heavenly gift and have been made partakers of the Holy Spirit, and have tasted the good word of God and the powers of the age to come, and then have fallen away, it is impossible to renew them again to repentance, since they crucify to themselves the Son of God, and put Him to open shame" (Hebrews 6:4-6).

This is a warning for Christians—those who have actually been made partakers of the Holy Spirit. Christians can fall away, and when they reach a certain point it is impossible for them to repent and return to God, having been hardened by the deceitfulness of sin (Hebrews 3:13). God has created Christians to do good works (Ephesians 2:10), but when all we yield is brambles and thorns instead of the peaceable fruit of righteousness, we shall be burned.

II Peter 2:20-22

Christians are warned of the dangers if this world by Peter: "For if after they have escaped the defilements of the world by the knowledge of the Lord and Savior Jesus Christ, they are again entangled in them and are overcome, the last state has become worse for them than the first. For it would have been better for them not to have known the way of righteousness, than having known it, to turn away from the holy commandment delivered to them" (II Peter 2:20,21).

The world has many forms of entangling alliances whose net awaits the unwary Christian pilgrim. When one of God's saints becomes overcome by one of these myriads of death traps, the Scripture is very plain—it would have been better for him not to have known the way of righteousness. Dogs who return to their own vomit, clean pigs to their mire—pity the Christian who turns back to his former way of life.

Galatians 5:4

"You have been severed from Christ, you who are seeking to be justified by law; you have fallen from grace" (Galatians 5:4).

There are those who contend today that once a person is in God's grace, he cannot fall from it. Galatians 5:4 ought to be plain enough to prove to anyone who accepts the Bible as God's final word that one can be a part of Christ, and then sever that relationship. Such severance is plainly called "falling from grace."

Summary

A Christian must remain faithful until death. He must meet the obstacles in his path and overcome them. "Be faithful until death, and I will give you the crown of life." (Revelation 2:10).

SUMMARY OF ENTIRE LESSON

In our study of God's plan of salvation, we have covered these main points:

1. Our problem is that our own sins condemn us to hell.
2. The good news—the gospel—is that Jesus died for our sins.
3. We answered the question "What must I do?" and found that we must:
    a) Believe that Jesus is the Christ, and that He was raised from the dead.
    b) Repent.
    c) Confess with the mouth that Jesus is Lord.
    d) Be immersed (in water) into Christ for the forgiveness of our sins.
4. Repentance includes an actual change in behavior.
5. Baptism is immersion in water, and it is essential to salvation. There is only one acceptable immersion—that is immer-

sion into Christ through the medium of water as a result of an individual's own desire to obey the gospel.

6. If a person refuses to do God's will, he will burn forever; if he does God's will, he will live forever!

7. The Christian must remain faithful until death.

GOD'S PLAN OF SALVATION

Instructions: *This set of questions is divided into two sections— Specific Questions and General Questions. The specific questions bring out many details in the study, and help you to understand many of the important points, and where in scripture to find answers to many common questions. The general questions help you pick out the major ideas and concepts in the study. You may use your Bible and study booklet for the Specific Questions, but try to answer the General Questions from memory.*

Each section is divided into subsections, each of which has its own type of questions and its attendant instructions.

Specific Questions

True or False?

_____ 1. Jesus said, "I am the way, and the truth, and the life: however, one may come to the Father other than by Me."

_____ 2. Paul proclaimed that the times of ignorance were past.

_____ 3. God has proven the He will judge the world in righteousness by raising Jesus from the dead.

_____ 4. When Jesus is revealed from heaven, He will deal out punishment to those who do not obey the gospel, but He will have mercy on those who didn't know about God.

_____ 5. Each of us must have an Advocate with the Father, Jesus Christ the righteous.

Multiple choice. More than one answer may be correct; show all correct answers.

_____ 1. The problem that all men face is:
a) They have sinned.
b) The devil made me do it.
c) Man's sins separate him from God.
d) Eternal fire is the punishment for committing sin.

_____ 2. Sin is:
a) Fun
b) Rebellion against God

c) Disobedience to God
d) Okay in small amounts

_____ 3. Adam and Eve:
a) Were both deceived by the serpent
b) Ate the forbidden fruit
c) Sinned by disobeying God
d) Hid from God after they sinned

_____ 4. Death:
a) In the Bible usually means spiritual separation from God
b) Means separation
c) Came upon Adam immediately after he ate the fruit, even though he lived in the body 930 years
d) In a physical way came upon all mankind as a result of Adam's sin

_____ 5. That sin separates man from God is clearly expressed in:
a) Hezekiah 12:1
b) Isaiah 59:1,2
c) James 1:13-16
d) John 9:31

_____ 6. Scriptures which make it clear that all are guilty of sins are:
a) Romans 3:23
b) Galatians 3:22
c) Psalm 51:5
d) Romans 8:1

_____ 7. Small children:
a) Cannot inherit the sins of their father (Ezekiel 18:20)
b) Inherit Adam's original sin
c) Follow Paul's example: There was a time when he was without sin, then the Law came and he died spiritually
d) Are to be converted and become like children

_____ 8. The penalty for sin:
a) Is a slap on the hands
b) Is eternal death, which is as long as eternal life.
c) Is something we deserve
d) Is hell

9. Threat of eternal punishment:
   a) Doesn't work
   b) Would never be used by a loving God
   c) Forces man toward faith in Jesus
   d) Causes us to break our will to serve King Jesus

10. Talking about sin and its consequences:
    a) Is negative
    b) Is Biblical
    c) Is a Puritanical myth
    d) Is un-Christian

Matching.

____ 1.	All have sinned and fall short of the glory of God	a) Romans 7:9
____ 2.	Shut up in a jailhouse	b) Matthew 21:44
____ 3.	The day that you eat, you shall surely die	c) Ezekiel 18:20
____ 4.	Your iniquities have made a separation between you and your God	d) John 14:6
		e) Genesis 2:16,17
		f) James 1:13-16
		g) Matthew 25:46
____ 5.	Small children are innocent of sin	h) Isaiah 59:1,2
		i) Romans 3:23
		j) Galatians 3:22
____ 6.	Eternal punishment	
____ 7.	Will broken to Savior's	
____ 8.	Sin brings forth death	
____ 9.	Sin is not inherited	
____ 10.	The way to the Father	

Explain how Romans 7:9 shows that small children are innocent of sin.

_____
_____
_____
_____
_____
_____
_____
_____
_____

Fill in the blanks.

1. The word *gospel* means _____ _____ or _____ _____. Its Greek equivalent is _____.

2. Paul said that the basic elements of the gospel were that _____ _____ _____ _____ according to the Scriptures, and that he was _____, and that He was _____ _____ _____ _____ _____ according to the Scriptures.

3. The instructions for the Jewish Passover are given first in _____ 12. Jesus Christ is our Passover Lamb according to _____ 5:7. The Passover represented God's passing _____ the houses where the blood of a _____ had been sprinkled when God destroyed the _____ _____ of man and beast in the land of Egypt.

4. The Day of _____ was a major Israelite religious rite. On this day the _____ Priest sprinkled the blood of _____ for his own sins, followed by the blood of a _____ for the sins of the people in the back room of the tabernacle (called the Holy of Holies). Then he confessed the sins of the people as he laid his hands on the head of another _____. This animal was then led into the wilderness and turned loose, and it was given the name _____. This is recorded in Leviticus 16:1-34.

5. It is made clear in _____ 10:4 that the blood of bulls and goats cannot forgive sins. For this reason it was necessary that Jesus shed His blood on the cross as described in _____ _____.

6. According to Law, _____ _____ _____ of blood _____ _____ _____ _____. Therefore it was necessary for the _____ of the things in the heavens (the Israelite tabernacle and instruments of service) to be cleansed with the blood of animal sacrifices, but the heavenly things themselves (all things connected with the church) with _____ _____ than these. The blood of _____ is the offering of better sacrifices than these Old Testament offerings.

7. Christ appeared as a _____ _____ of the good things ____ _____, and He entered through the greater and more perfect tabernacle, _____ _____ _____ _____, that is to say, not of this creation (the church, in other words, which is a spiritual building, not a physical building—Ephesians 2:19-22). Not through the _____ of goats and calves, but

45

through _____ _____ _____, He entered the holy place
_____ _____ _____.

8. The blood of Christ can _____ _____
   _____ from dead works to serve the living God.

9. Christ became a _____ for us to redeem us from the
   curse of the Law. The curse of the Law is _____
   _____. _____ _____ kept the command-
   ments of the Law, except Jesus, so He _____ us
   from the curse by _____ on the tree for us.

10.
   "_____
   _____
   _____
   _____." (John 3:16)

True or False?

_____ 1. The word *evangel* is a Latin word meaning "good news,"
and is the word translated "gospel" in most English versions of the Bible.

_____ 2. All the Old Testament sacrifices pointed forward to the
perfect sacrifice of the Son of God Himself.

_____ 3. Christ is the Christian's Passover Lamb.

_____ 4. The good news is that Christ died for our sins, that He was
buried, and that He was raised on the third day.

_____ 5. The Israelite celebration of the Passover comes from the 12
tribes passing over the Red Sea on dry ground.

_____ 6. Christ's blood was shed in order to solve our problem (that
our own sins condemn us to eternal punishment).

_____ 7. Christ is the Christian's High Priest.

_____ 8. The Old Testament High Priesthood and its sacrifices
pointed forward to the High Priesthood of Christ and His
sacrifice.

_____ 9. The Old Testament High Priest offered the blood of a male
goat for the sins of the people in the back room of the tabernacle (the tent of meeting).

_____10. Jesus, the High Priest of the New Testament, offered His
own blood in the true Holy of Holies—Heaven.

_____11. It is impossible for the blood of bulls and goats to forgive
sins.

_____12. The good news of the shed blood is that through the blood
of Christ God promises a clean conscience to the Christian,

something that was not obtainable in the Old Testament.

_____13. "Redeem" means "buy back."

_____14. Jesus redeemed us from the curse of the Law.

_____15. Jesus hung on the tree (cross) to buy us back after being lost through our being unable to keep the commandments of the Law.

_____16. The reason that we have any good news at all is that God loved each of us enough to send His Son to die for us.

Matching.

_____ 1. Good news   a) Church

_____ 2. Passover   b) There is no forgiveness

_____ 3. Day of Atonement   c) I Corinthians 15:3,4

_____ 4. High Priest   d) Heaven

_____ 5. Blood of bulls and goats   e) Blood of Christ

_____ 6. Tabernacle   f) Behold the Lamb of God

_____ 7. Curse of the Law   g) Scapegoat

_____ 8. Holy of Holies   h) Christ

_____ 9. Without the shedding of blood   i) Redemption center

_____10. The cross   j) Hung on a tree

Compare the New Testament with the will of a rich man, particularly explaining the time at which the will takes effect.

_____

_____

_____

_____

Multiple choice. More than one answer may be correct; show all correct answers.

_____ 1. The new covenant:
   a) Began with Christ's death
   b) Is Christ's will for us today
   c) Took effect after the thief on the cross was pardoned
   d) Is referred to in Hebrews 9:16,17

_____ 2. Jesus:
   a) Said that the scripture cannot be broken
   b) Made a sacrifice so complete that all men will go to

47

heaven
c) Had authority on earth to forgive sins
d) Pardoned the thief on the cross as His first act under the New Covenant

_____ 3.   Under the New Covenant, the following are required for salvation:
a) Belief in Jesus
b) Repentance
c) Confession that Jesus is Lord
d) Immersion in water

_____ 4.   The gospel:
a) Is limited to Christ's death
b) Contains commands to be obeyed
c) Must be obeyed or the individual who does not will go to hell
d) Guarantees that no one will perish

_____ 5.   The Philippian jailer:
a) Was a descendent of Philip of Macedon
b) Had his story told in Acts 16
c) Believed in Jesus as the Son of God immediately when Paul told him to
d) Believed and was immersed after he heard the gospel preached

_____ 6.   The 3000 on the day of Pentecost:
a) Were told to repent and accept Jesus into their hearts
b) Were told to repent and be immersed for the forgiveness of their sins
c) Obeyed the gospel
d) Were told to save themselves from their wicked generation

_____ 7.   The Ethiopian Eunuch:
a) Was a Jew
b) Was reading from the prophet Isaiah
c) Wanted to be immersed as a result of Philip preaching Jesus to him
d) Went down into the water and was immersed after he confessed with his mouth that Jesus was the Christ

_____ 8. The man named Saul:
   a) Was saved on the Damascus Road
   b) Was later known as the apostle Paul
   c) Had his sins washed away three days after he met Jesus on the Damascus Road
   d) Had to be immersed because he was such a terrible persecutor of the church. We don't need to be immersed today.

_____ 9. No one can be saved:
   a) Unless he believes
   b) Unless he repents
   c) Unless he confesses Jesus as Lord
   d) Unless he is immersed for the forgiveness of his sins

_____ 10. God's ways:
   a) Are ridiculous
   b) Are without partiality
   c) Are higher than man's ways
   d) Are incomprehensible

True or False?

_____ 1. He who believes and is baptized shall be saved; he who does not believe shall be condemned.
_____ 2. We must all repent or we shall all perish.
_____ 3. God is not willing that any should perish, but that we all come to repentance.
_____ 4. When we accept Jesus into our hearts, we are immediately saved.
_____ 5. The Philippian jailer and his household were immersed immediately when they believed the gospel.
_____ 6. Jesus will deal out punishment to those who do not know God and to those who do not obey the gospel.
_____ 7. All of us must repent and be immersed in the name of Jesus for the forgiveness of our sins and to receive the gift of the Holy Spirit.
_____ 8. God shows no partiality.
_____ 9. We must be immersed to wash away our sins.
_____ 10. Acts 8:37 really doesn't belong in the Bible.
_____ 11. Romans 10:9,10 makes it clear that confession with the mouth preceded salvation.
_____ 12. The example of the apostles is our guide for today under the

New Covenant.

_____ 13. Hearing comes before faith; a person must hear the word preached in order to believe.

_____ 14. According to John 10:35, God will not deviate from what He has written in the Bible.

_____ 15. Even if a person is on the Sahara Desert, God requires him to be immersed for the forgiveness of his sins in order to go to heaven.

Matching.

_____ 1. The New Will   a) Acts 16:16-34
_____ 2. God's ways   b) Luke 23:39-43
_____ 3. The Philippian jailer   c) Hebrews 9:16,17
_____ 4. The 3000 on the day of   d) Mark 2:1-12
      Pentecost   e) Acts 22:1-16
_____ 5. The Ethiopian Eunuch   f) Isaiah 55:8-11
_____ 6. Saul of Tarsus   g) II Thessalonians 1:8
_____ 7. Obey the gospel   h) Acts 2:36-42
_____ 8. The thief on the Cross   i) Acts 8:26-40
_____ 9. The paralyzed man   j) Romans 2:11
_____ 10. God shows no partiality

Fill in the blanks.

1. Many people have their own _____ of what constitutes repentance. We are anxious to find _____ definition of repentance.

2. Jesus said, "Unless you _____, you will all likewise _____."

3. An excellent example of repentance is found in the Old Testament book of _____. God sent the prophet to the city of _____.

4. The people of Nineveh were _____ in God's eyes. Jonah told them, "Yet _____ days, and _____ will be overthrown."

5. The Assyrians were called upon to _____ from their wicked ways by the _____. He had hope that God would withdraw His _____ _____.

6. When God saw their _____, He did not bring the calamity He promised upon _____.

7. Jesus said that the people of Nineveh _____ at the

preaching of Jonah.

8. Jesus' definition of repentance is _____ _____
_____ _____.

9. Sorrow according to the will of God produces _____.
10. Sorrow of this world produces _____.
11. Peter is an example of sorrow producing _____.
Judas Iscariot is an example of sorrow producing
_____.

12. Mere sorrow is _____ repentance.
13. Repentance is _____ _____ _____ _____
_____ _____ _____ _____ _____
_____ _____ _____.

14. If there is no change, there is no _____.

True or False?

_____ 1. Baptism is not controversial.

_____ 2. Baptism is not controversial because it is not important.

_____ 3. If something is confusing, most people just don't get involved in trying to find out what the truth is.

_____ 4. It is not important what any denomination teaches about
baptism. What is important is what God teaches about
baptism.

_____ 5. The Greek word *rantizo,* which means "to sprinkle," is the
word translated "baptize" in most common English versions of the Bible.

_____ 6. The Greek word *baptizo,* which means "to immerse," is the
word transliterated "baptize" in most common English versions of the Bible.

_____ 7. The Old Testament was written in, and translated from,
the Greek language.

_____ 8. God said *immerse* as clearly as He could say it in the Greek
language. He said *baptizo.*

_____ 9. We can learn what God means in using a certain word by
how He uses it in context.

_____ 10. The example of the saddle horse and the saw horse illustrates the use of context in determining the meaning of a
word.

_____ 11. John the Baptist was baptizing at Aenon near Salim because there was much water there.

_____ 12. After He was baptized, Jesus Himself went up immediately
from the water.

_____ 13. When the Ethiopian Eunuch was baptized, both he and Philip went down into the water, as one would have to do if the Ethiopian were being immersed.

_____ 14. It was not until 1311 A.D., at the Council of Ravenna, that the Roman Catholic Church decreed that sprinkling and pouring (effusion) were of equal validity with immersion.

Study carefully the chart entitled REQUIREMENTS OF NEW TESTA-MENT BAPTISM. Then reproduce the chart from memory.

True or False?

_____ 1. In Acts 2:38, in answer to the people's question about what they must do, Peter answered, "Repent, and put all your trust in Jesus to save you from your sins."

_____ 2. In Acts 2:38, in answer to the people's question about what they must do, Peter answered, "Repent, and accept Jesus into your heart, and you will be saved."

_____ 3. In Acts 2:38, in answer to the people's question about what they must do, Peter answered, "There is nothing you can do to be saved. You must simply trust Jesus to save you, and He will."

_____ 4. In Acts 2:38, in answer to the people's question about what they must do, Peter answered, "Repent, and let each of you be immersed in the name of Jesus Christ for the forgiveness of you sins, and you shall receive the gift of the Holy Spirit."

_____ 5. "In the name of Jesus" means "by the authority of Jesus."

_____ 6. In James 2:24, the Holy Spirit makes it clear that a person may be justified by "faith alone."

_____ 7. In Ephesians 2:8,9, the apostle Paul makes it clear that we are saved through faith, and that our good works by themselves do not justify us before God.

_____ 8. Many religious groups today teach that immersion in water is a work which follows salvation.

_____ 9. The Bible makes it clear that immersion in water is for the forgiveness of sin.

_____ 10. Matthew 26:28 shows that the words "forgiveness of sins" tell the reason why something is done. Jesus' blood was shed in order that we may have our sins forgiven; we are to be immersed in order that we may have our sins forgiven.

_____ 11. In Acts 8:35, Philip "preached Jesus" to the Ethiopian. Immersion in water is part of preaching Jesus.

_____ 12. In Acts 10:47,48, we can clearly see that immersion in Jesus' name occurs in water.

_____ 13. Both repentance and immersion in Jesus' name are both requirements for the forgiveness of sins.

Multiple choice. More than one answer may be correct; show all correct answers.

_____ 1. In Romans 6, the question that Paul is discussing is: "How shall we as Christians, who have died to the practice of sin, still live in sin?" In that connection he points out:
   a) When we were immersed into Christ, we were immersed into Christ's death.
   b) We were buried with Christ by accepting Him into our hearts, then we were immersed as an outward sign of an inward grace that we already possess.
   c) We were buried with Christ in immersion.
   d) We were raised from immersion to walk in newness of life.

_____ 2. There is no condemnation for those who are in Christ Jesus (Romans 8:1). What two verses of scripture tell us how to enter into Christ?
   a) John 1:12
   b) Galatians 3:27
   c) Romans 6:3
   d) Colossians 2:6

3. Man-made perversion of the gospel is declared to be:
   a) Accursed
   b) Anathema
   c) Wonderful
   d) Okay

4. The only way through the doorway of salvation is:
   a) Sprinkling
   b) Singing Alleluiah
   c) Blessing God
   d) Immersion into Christ

5. We contact the blood of Christ, God's sin-cleansing agent:
   a) In immersion into Christ
   b) In repentance and immersion in Christ's name
   c) In Sunday school
   d) In being a "nice guy"

6. Being "born again" is described in:
   a) John 3:3-5
   b) Romans 6:4
   c) Being buried with Christ and resurrected to walk in new-
      ness of life
   d) Going back into a mother's womb

7. Union with Christ occurs:
   a) In the likeness of Jesus' death
   b) As described in Romans 6:5
   c) In immersion in water
   d) With the laying-on-of-hands of one of the priesthood

8. To be resurrected with Christ means:
   a) At some time in the future we will be resurrected from
      the dead
   b) The new man is now to be as Christ was after He was
      raised from the dead
   c) We will all go out in the rapture
   d) Something only figurative with no real meaning for
      today's enlightened generation

9. In immersion:
   a) A sign is given to unbelievers that this one being im-
      mersed is already saved

b) The old man is crucified
c) The body of sin is resurrected
d) The sinful nature is buried

_____ 10. When Christ was raised from the dead:
   a) The devil had no way to even try to tempt Christ, for He had destroyed the power of the devil in rising from the dead
   b) Death no longer was master over Him
   c) He would from that point on live to God
   d) He was subject to death in the next world

_____ 11. We are to think of ourselves:
   a) As being exceedingly sinful
   b) As imperfect human beings
   c) As being essentially the same after our immersion as before
   d) As being as Christ was when He was raised from the dead

Fill in the blanks.

1. Christians are the sons of God _____ _____ in Christ Jesus. He becomes a son of God by being _____ _____ Christ, at which point he is _____ with Christ.
2. Many religious groups who believe that an individual is saved by _____ _____ have trouble reconciling Ephesians 2:8,9 with _____ _____.
3. To many people, immersion is a _____ which follows one's salvation.
4. The Bible clearly teaches that _____ is a part of faith.
5. A person going to a costume party may be clothed with Donald Duck by putting on a Donald Duck costume. An individual is clothed with _____ _____ by being _____ into Christ.
6. By one Spirit we were all immersed _____ _____ _____. Another name for the body is the _____. Immersion into the body of Christ occurs in _____.
7. Colossians 2:12 also mentions that we were _____ with Christ _____ _____. Not only that, but we were also _____ up with Him.
8. Immersion into Christ is not a work that one might do to save himself. In immersion, _____ does all the work, and we must have

55

_____ in that working.

True or False?

____ 1. In Romans 6:17,18, the expression "having been freed from sin" tips us off that Paul is talking about immersion.

____ 2. Having been "obedient from the heart to that *form* of teaching" means that there are different teachings that one may hear from the different denominations, and Paul was thankful that we obeyed the one that we happened to hear.

____ 3. The word "form" means "mold" or "likeness."

____ 4. The basic teaching, or doctrine, of Christ is His death, burial, and resurrection.

____ 5. Immersion into Christ in water is the likeness of the death, burial, and resurrection of Christ.

____ 6. We must be obedient to the likeness of Jesus' death, burial, and resurrection from our own hearts.

____ 7. Infants can obey the form of the basic doctrine of Christ, and by being obedient by their own choice are made free from original sin.

____ 8. Of first importance in the gospel is that Christ died for our sins, that He was buried, and that He was raised from the dead on the third day.

____ 9. According to I Peter 3:21, immersion now saves us.

____ 10. As the waters of the flood served to destroy the earth and save Noah, so the waters of immersion serve to destroy the old man and to save the new.

____ 11. Immersion saves us by the resurrection of Christ.

____ 12. Only God's grace saves a person, there is nothing that he can or must do in his own behalf.

____ 13. Immersion is a appeal to God for a clean conscience.

____ 14. Old Testament sacrifices and rituals could make a person clean in conscience.

____ 15. Being "born again" means being "born of water and Spirit."

____ 16. Immersion in Jesus' name includes both water and Spirit, according to Acts 2:38.

____ 17. A person enters the kingdom of God upon being born of water and Spirit.

____ 18. The kingdom of God is the church.

____ 19. When Jesus said, "He who believes in Me, from his innermost being shall flow rivers of living water," He was speaking of the Holy Spirit, who was not given until after Jesus' death.

_____ 20. *Washing* of regeneration in Titus 3:5 may be translated *bath* of regeneration.

_____ 21. A person is regenerated in immersion; he is continually renewed after his immersion by the Holy Spirit.

_____ 22. The church is cleansed, individually, by the bath of water and the word.

_____ 23. Peter says that one is born again by the living and abiding word of God.

_____ 24. One cannot be born again by both water and the word.

_____ 25. There is only one Lord—Jesus.

_____ 26. There is only one legitimate faith—Christian.

_____ 27. There is only one legitimate baptism—immersion into Christ through the medium of water.

_____ 28. According to Paul, immersion is not a part of preaching Jesus.

_____ 29. Few of the Corinthians were immersed.

_____ 30. Faith is more important than immersion because there are more Bible verses about faith than immersion.

_____ 31. Being born again is of little importance because there are so few Bible verses about it.

Multiple choice. More than one answer may be correct; show all correct answers.

_____ 1. When the Lord Jesus returns:
a) He will deal out punishment to those who do not know God
b) He will come with His angels
c) He will deal out punishment to those who do not obey the gospel
d) As a loving Savior, He will accept everyone at that time into His eternal home

_____ 2. If anyone's name is not found in the book of life, according to Revelation 20:15:
a) He simply never came back to life—he ceased to exist
b) He will be sent on to another world for a second chance
c) He is reincarnated in his effort to achieve Nirvana
d) He is cast into the lake of fire

_____ 3. If anyone does not have the Spirit of Christ:
a) He does not belong to Christ
b) He needs to repent and be immersed in the name of Christ

c) If he is a Christian, he really needs to change his attitude
d) He needs to accept Jesus into his heart

____ 4. According to John 3:17-21:
   a) Jesus came to save the world, not to condemn it
   b) Those who reject the Jesus of the Bible do so because they are evil
   c) Those who reject the Jesus of the Bible do so because they are ignorant
   d) Those who practice the truth always come to Jesus on His terms

____ 5. In Matthew 7:21:
   a) Jesus said that everyone who calls Him "Lord" will be saved
   b) Jesus said that only those who do God's will can enter the kingdom of heaven
   c) If you simply are sincere and do the best you know how, even if it's wrong, God will still have mercy on you
   d) Jesus said that not everyone who calls Him "Lord" will enter the kingdom of heaven

Matching.

____ 1. Cowardly, unbelieving, sorcer-   a) Hebrews 6:4-6
        ers, and liars go into the lake   b) Galatians 5:4
        of fire.   c) II Peter 2:20-22
____ 2. It is impossible to renew them   d) Revelation 21:1-8
        after they have tasted of the
        heavenly gift and have been
        partakers of the Holy Spirit,
        and then fall away.
____ 3. If a person becomes en-
        tangled in the defilements
        of the world and is overcome
        by them, his last state is
        worse than his first.
____ 4. A person may fall from
        grace.

General Questions

1. List the seven major sections of this study:
   a) _____
   b) _____
   c) _____
   d) _____
   e) _____
   f) _____
   g) _____
2. What is the problem that every person who is responsible for his own actions has with respect to God? _____
   _____
3. What does the word *gospel* mean? _____
   What is the gospel? _____
   _____
   _____

4. List the four initial requirements we must meet following our hearing the gospel in order to be saved:
   a) _____
   b) _____
   c) _____
   d) _____
5. Under which covenant do we live? _____ When did it take effect? _____
6. What example from the Old Testament clearly illustrates God's definition of repentance? _____
   _____
7. What is the meaning of the Greek word *baptizo?* _____
   _____
   This word is transliterated into what word in the English language?
   _____
8. What verse of scripture clearly shows that baptism is for forgiveness of sin? _____
9. What two verses of scripture show that a person enters into Jesus through immersion? _____
10. Immersion saves us by the _____ of Christ. It is an appeal to God for a _____ conscience (I Peter _____).
11. There is _____ Lord, _____ faith, _____ immersion.
12. Every person must make his choice—to _____ or _____ the gospel.

13. Refusal to obey the gospel results in _____ _____;
obedience to the gospel results in _____ _____.
14. That the Christian may go beyond the "point of no return" and be eternally lost is made clear in what verses of scripture? _____
_____
15. What scripture verse plainly states that a Christian can fall from grace? _____

True or False?

_____ 1. God will deal out punishment to those who don't know Him, and to those who do not obey the gospel of Jesus Christ.

_____ 2. The times of ignorance are past. God now requires all men to come to repentance.

_____ 3. God has shut up all men in the jailhouse of sin.

_____ 4. There was a time in Paul's life before the Law applied to him. This shows that small children are not held accountable for their actions.

_____ 5. Adam's death by eating the forbidden fruit was his separation from God. Physical death was a result of his separation from the tree of life.

_____ 6. The good news of Christianity is centered about Jesus' death, burial, and resurrection.

_____ 7. Immersion in water is the form of the teaching which we must obey to be freed from sin.

_____ 8. The New Testament went into effect with the birth of Jesus.

_____ 9. The thief on the cross was one of the first people saved under the terms of the new covenant.

_____ 10. The Philippian jailer believed and was immersed immediately upon his belief following the preaching of God's word to him.

_____ 11. Confession with the mouth that Jesus is Lord is essential to salvation.

_____ 12. Repentance is an actual change of behavior.

_____ 13. The Greek word *rantizo* means "to immerse."

_____ 14. A person repents and is immersed in the name of Jesus for the forgiveness of his sins, and to receive the gift of the Holy Spirit.

_____ 15. Those who hate the light will not come to Jesus on His terms.